GEOMETRICAL DESIGN COLORING BOOK

46 ORIGINAL DESIGNS BY
SPYROS HOREMIS

DOVER PUBLICATIONS, INC.
NEW YORK

PUBLISHER'S NOTE

The chances are that you have never before seen a coloring book anything like this one, which is filled with pure patterns and abstract shapes. Almost all coloring books consist of pictures of real things—of people, animals, plants and other familiar objects which one is expected to paint the correct—or at least a "reasonable"—color. Who ever heard of a blue strawberry?

How strange it is that people have not generally recognized that abstract patterns and shapes, which do not have any built-in color associations, allow us to "play" with color with absolute freedom. Here a "wrong" color choice is impossible, and we are limited only by our own imagination.

Although at first glance some of these designs may look very complicated, you will quickly discover that each one is made up of combinations of repeated shapes and parts. In each case you are free, of course, to use color to point up any aspect of the design that interests you. Some you will wish to tone down with a quiet and simple color scheme; others you will want to make as exciting and brilliant as a flashing neon sign. Whatever approach you choose, you can be sure that the finished picture will be uniquely your own, for no one else—not even the original artist—will have seen it exactly the way you have!

Published in Canada by General Publishing Company, Ltd., 30 Lesmill Road, Don Mills, Toronto, Ontario.
Published in the United Kingdom by Constable and Company, Ltd.

"Geometrical Design Coloring Book" is a new work, first published by Dover Publications, Inc., in 1973.

DOVER *Pictorial Archive* SERIES

This book belongs to the Dover Pictorial Archive Series. You may use the designs and illustrations for graphics and crafts applications, free and without special permission, provided that you include no more than ten in the same publication or project. (For permission for additional use, please write to Dover Publications, Inc., 31 East 2nd Street, Mineola, N.Y. 11501.)
However, republication or reproduction of any illustration by any other graphic service whether it be in a book or in any other design resource is strictly prohibited.

International Standard Book Number: 0-486-20180-5

Manufactured in the United States of America
Dover Publications, Inc.
31 East 2nd Street
Mineola, N.Y. 11501

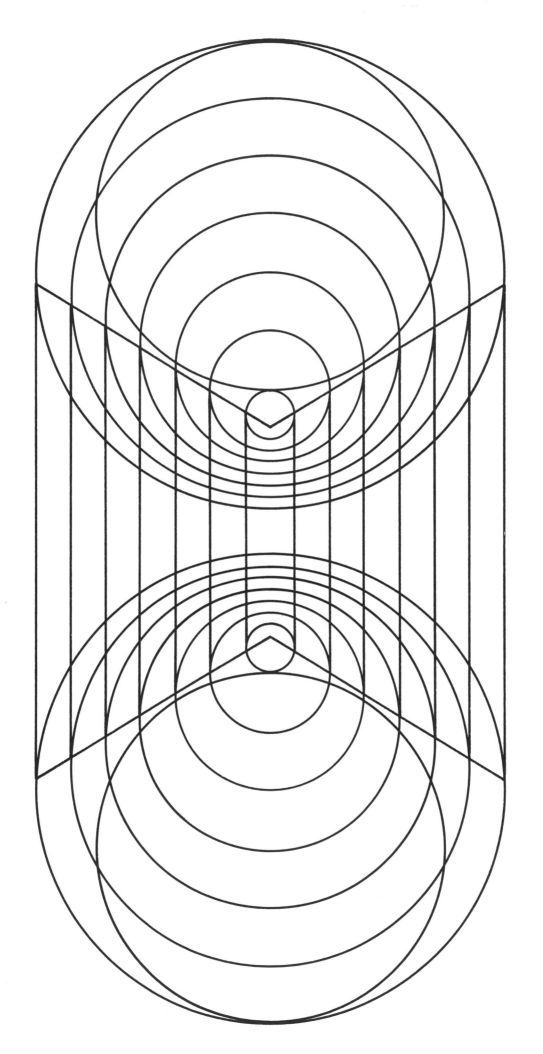

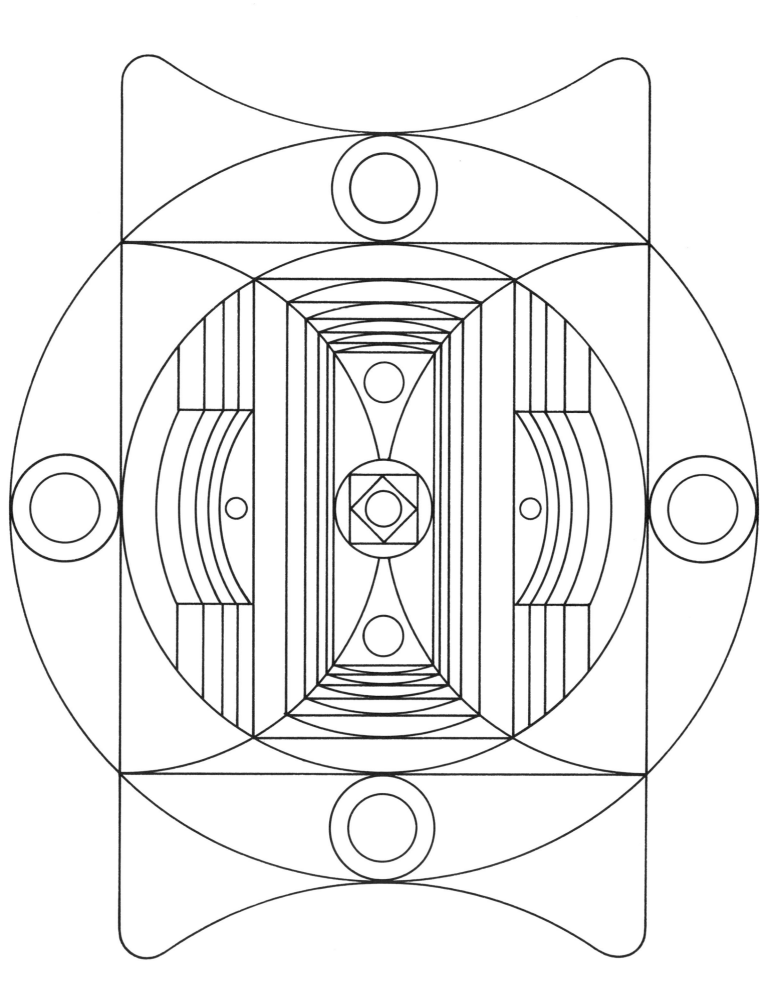

3

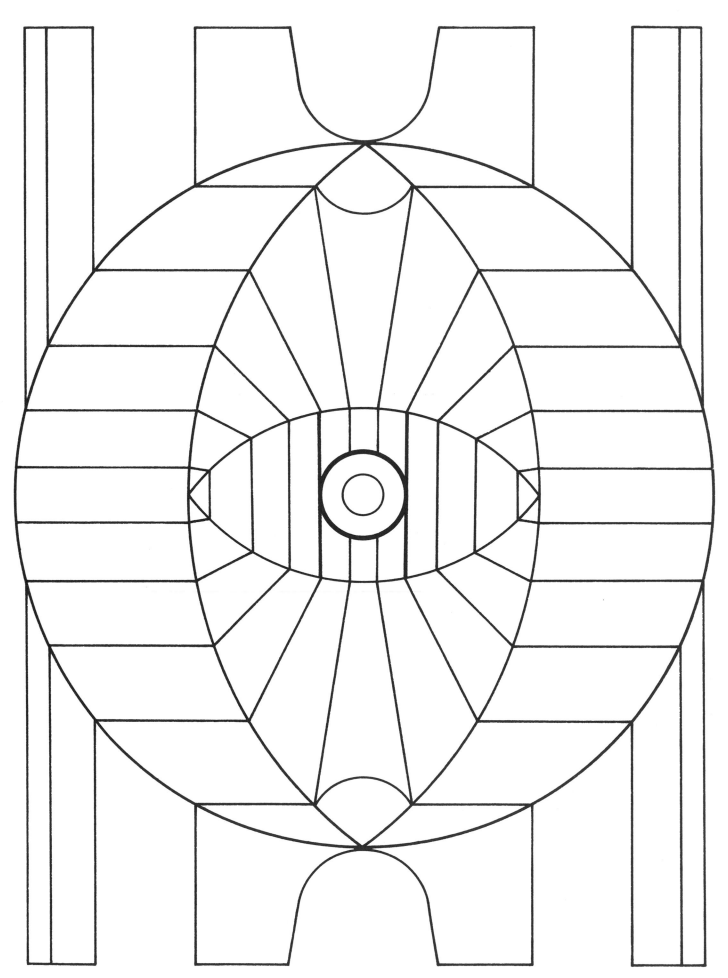

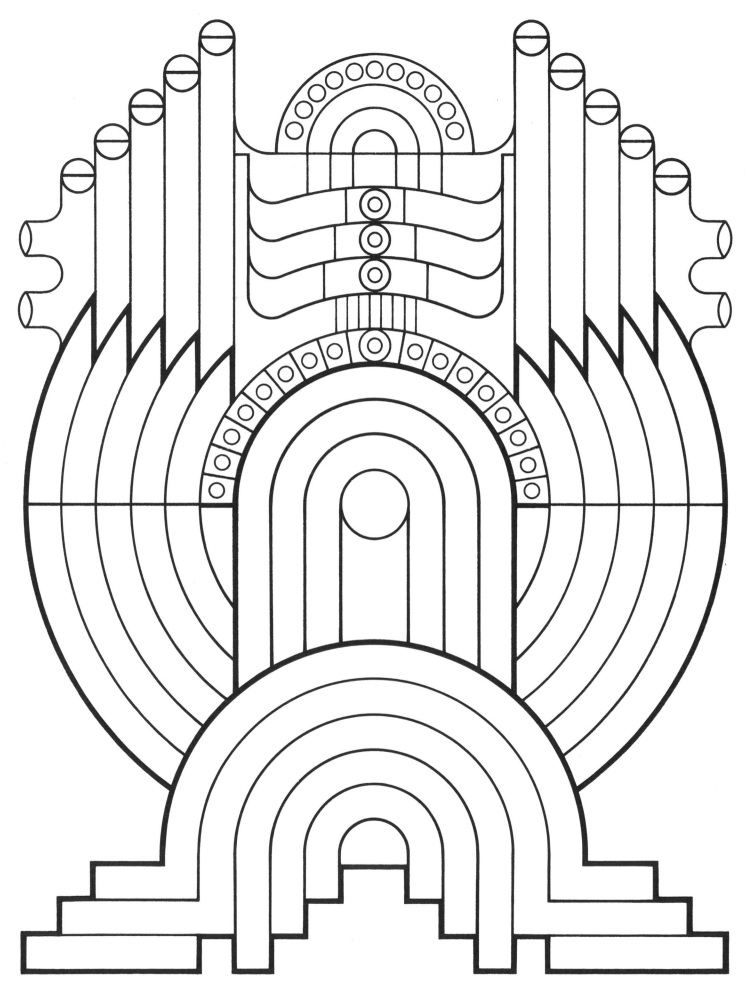

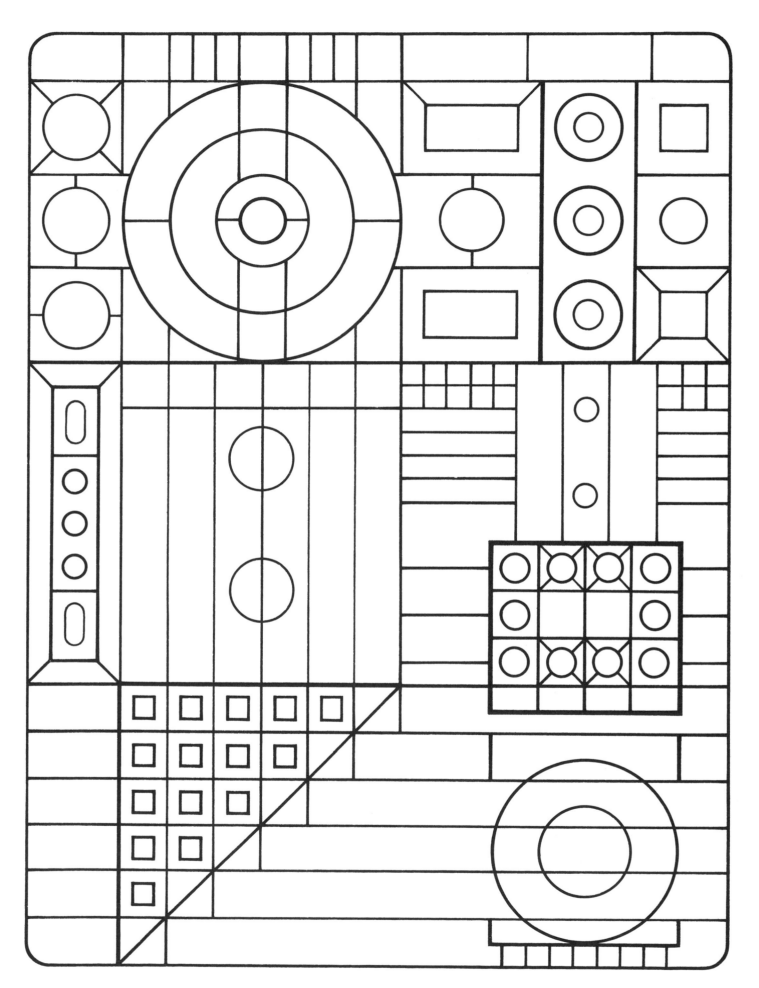

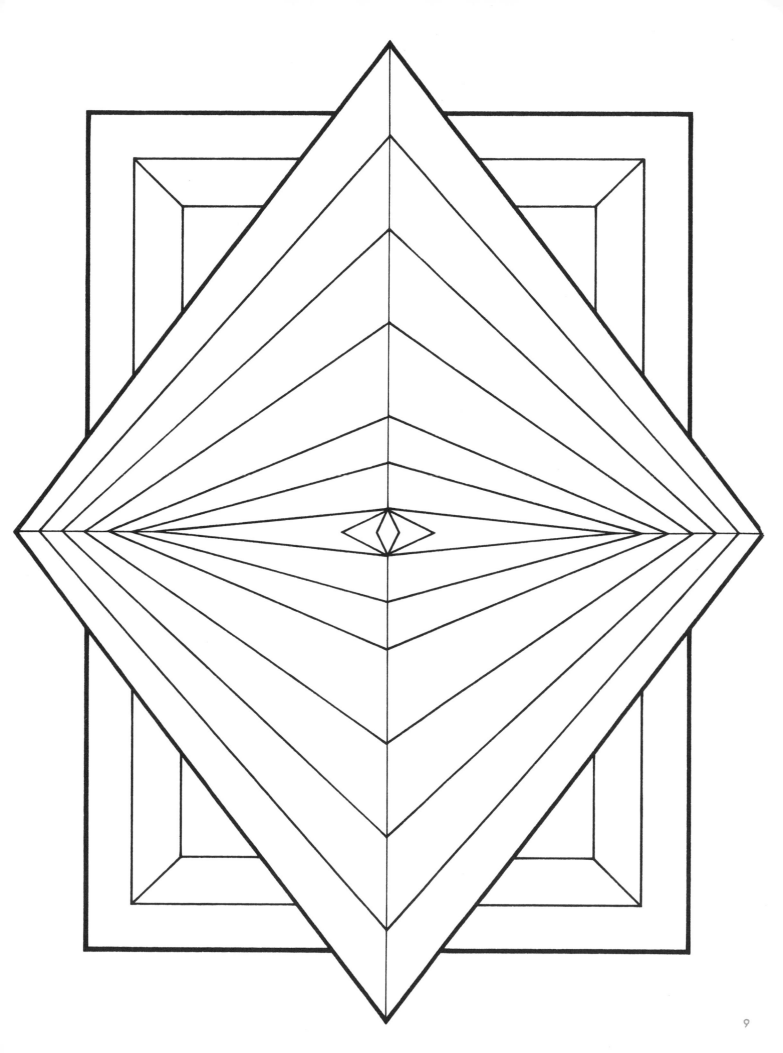

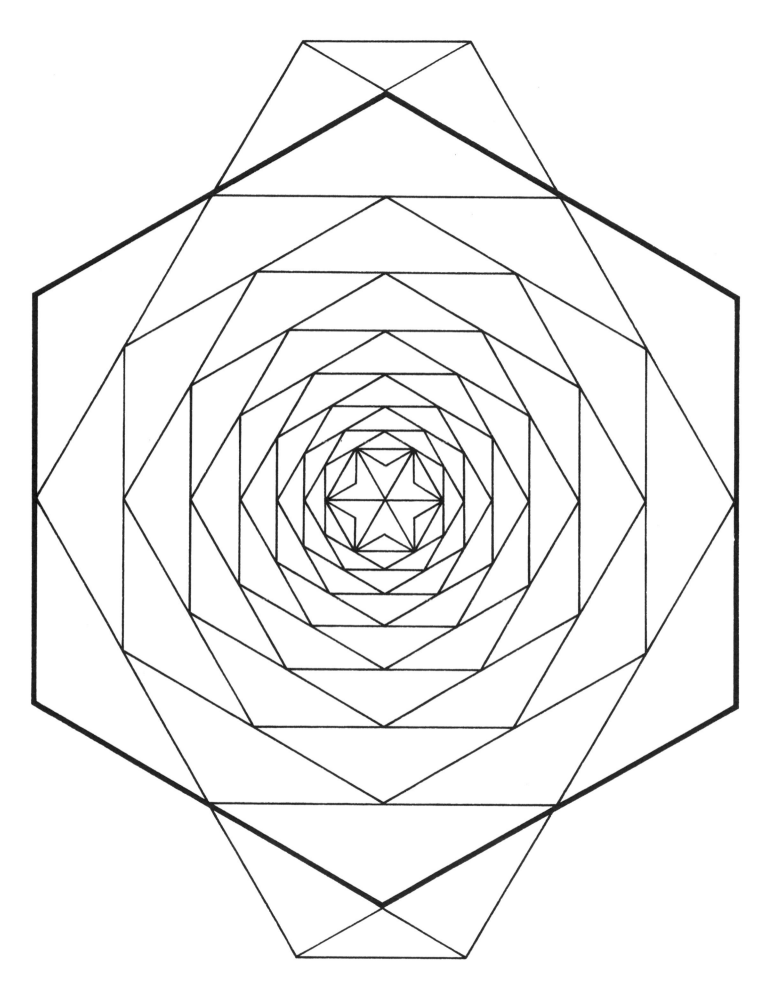

13

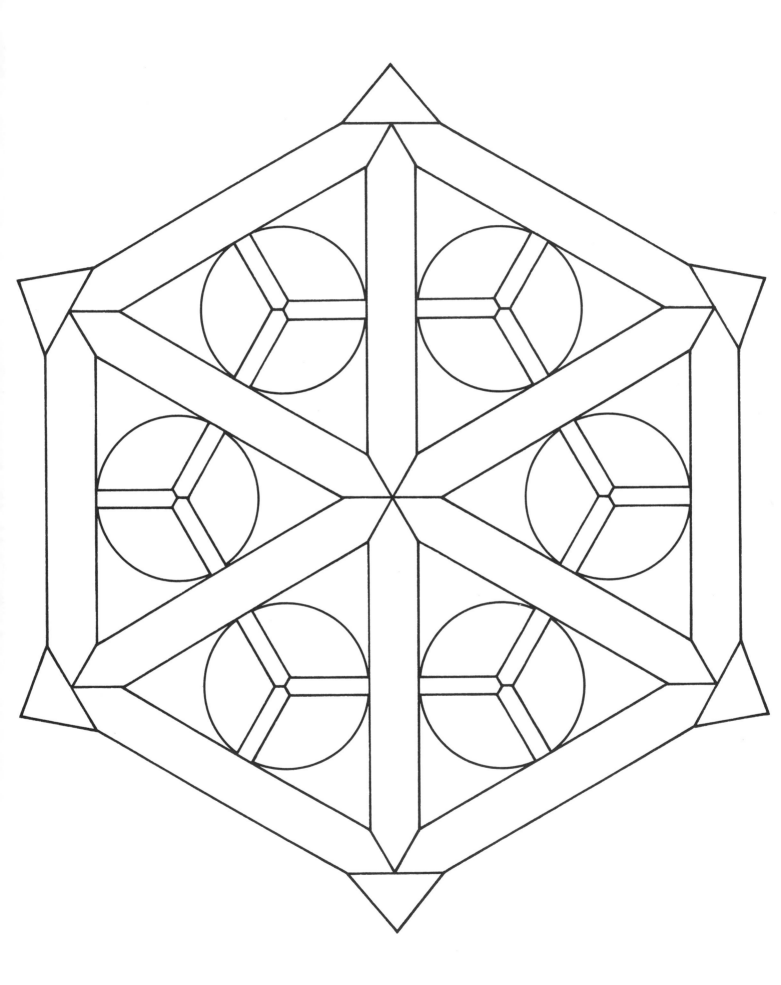

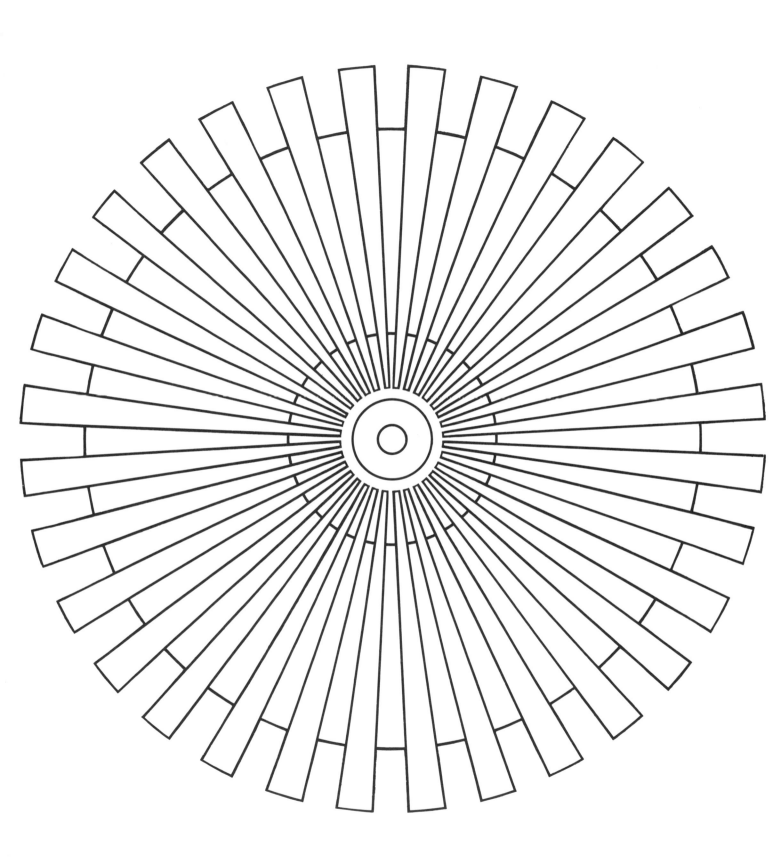

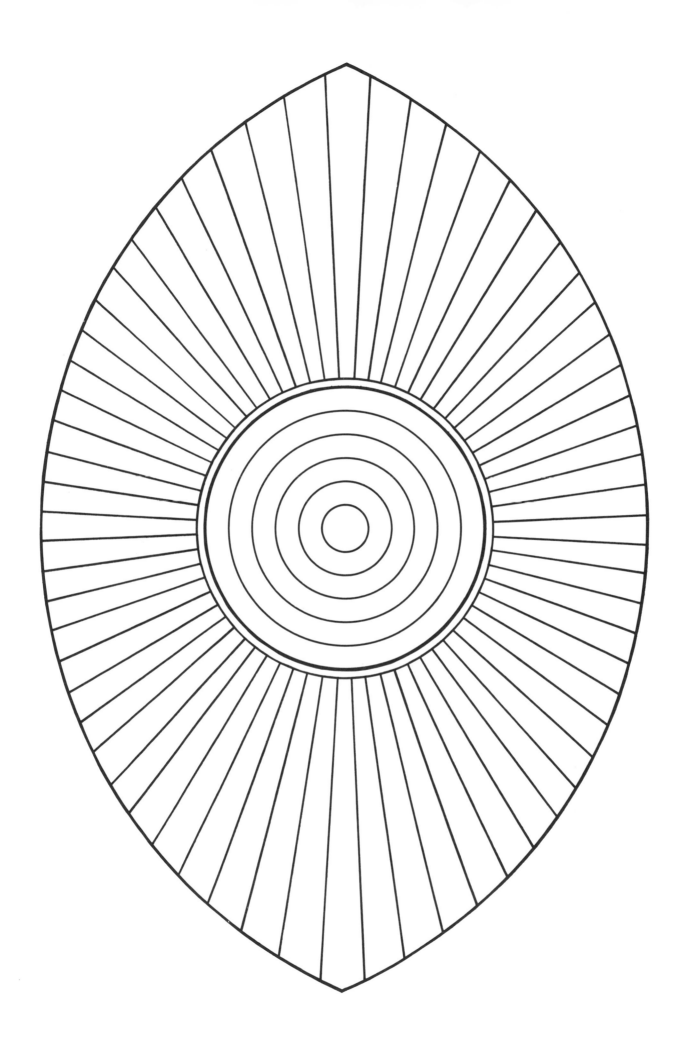

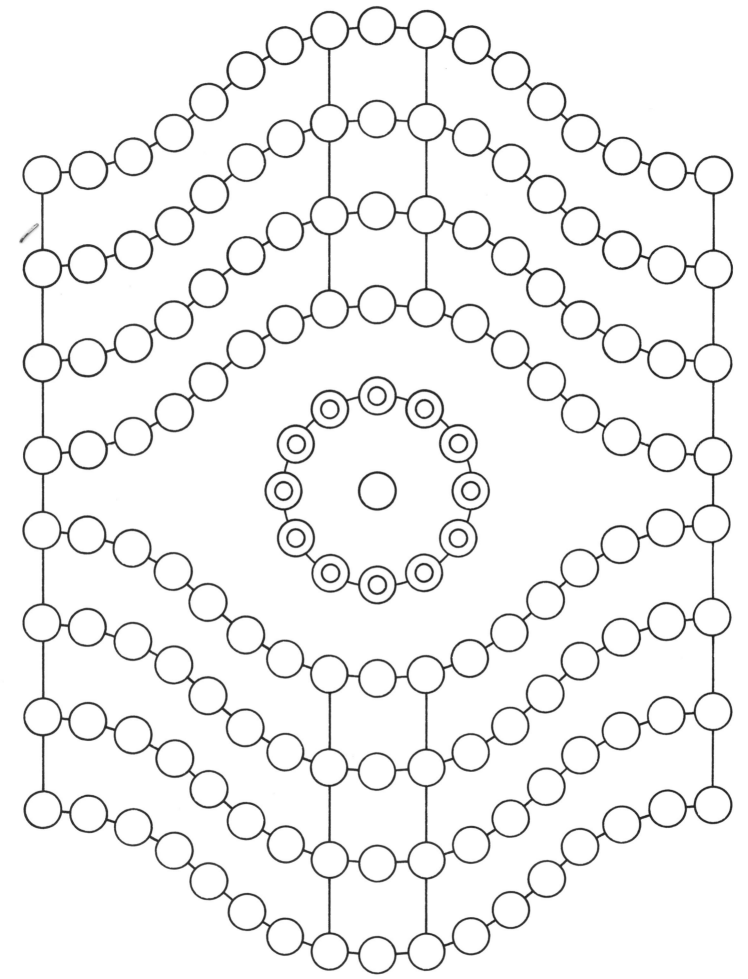

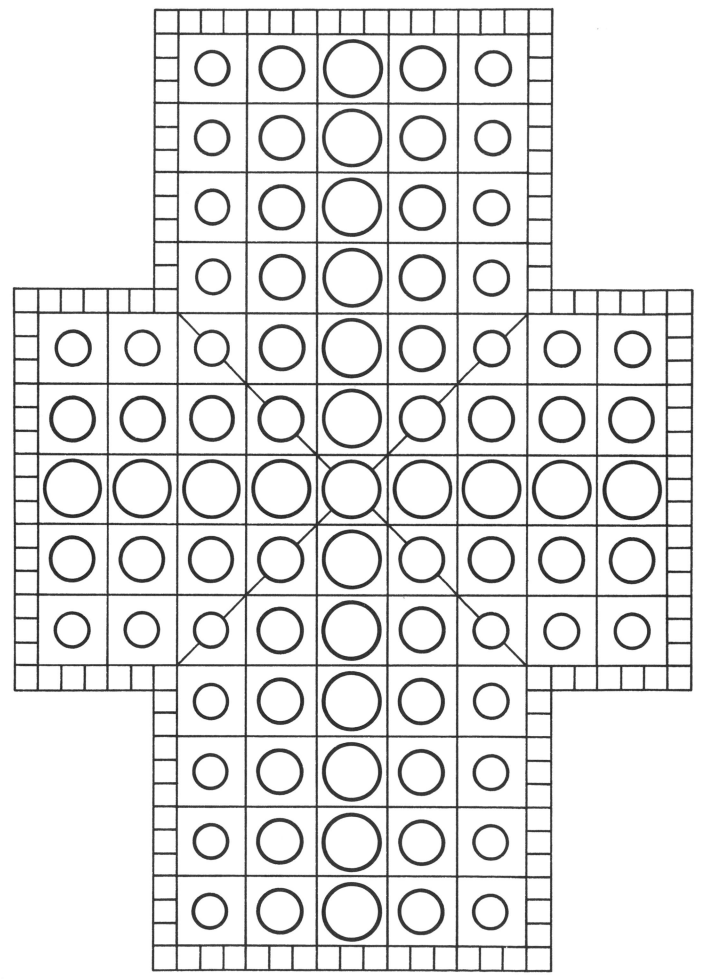

26

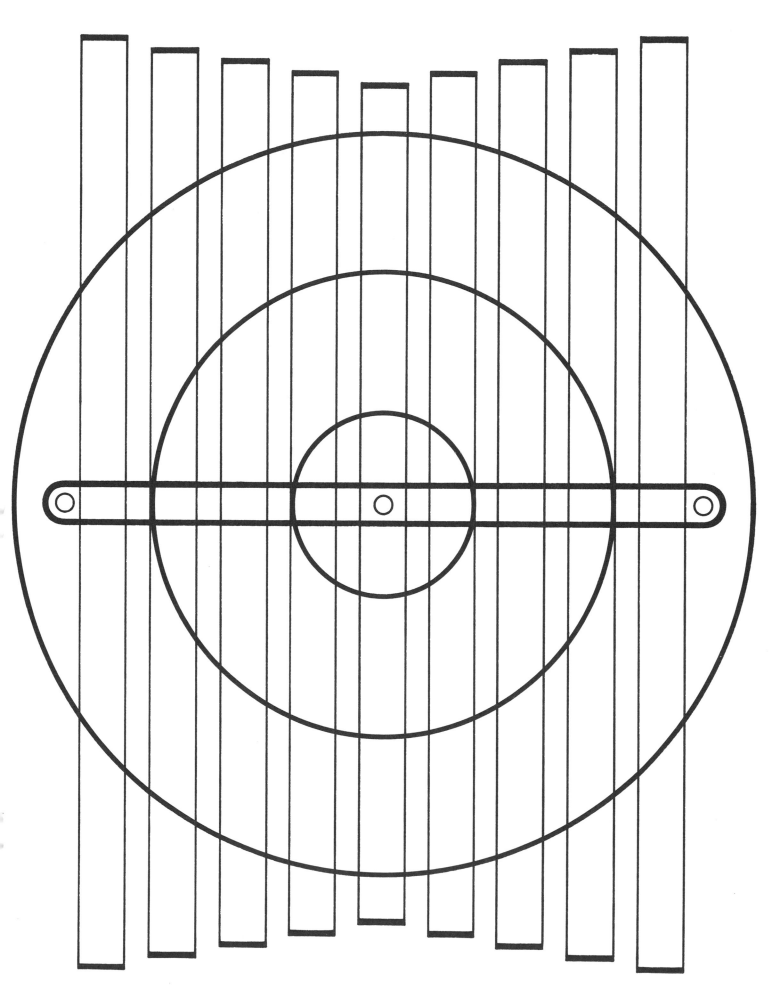

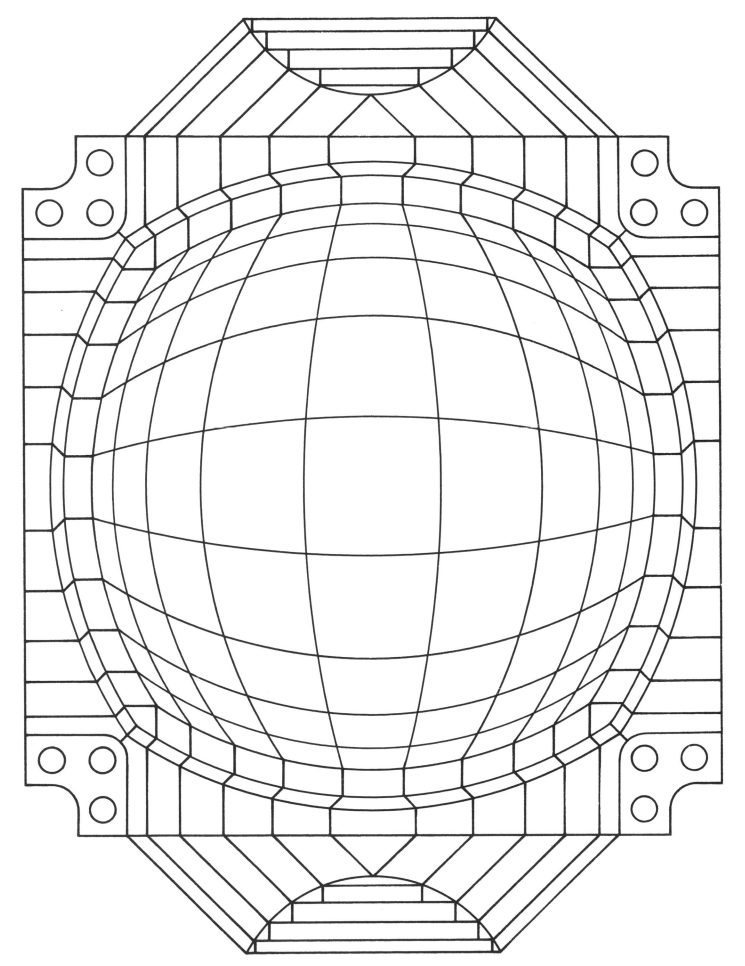

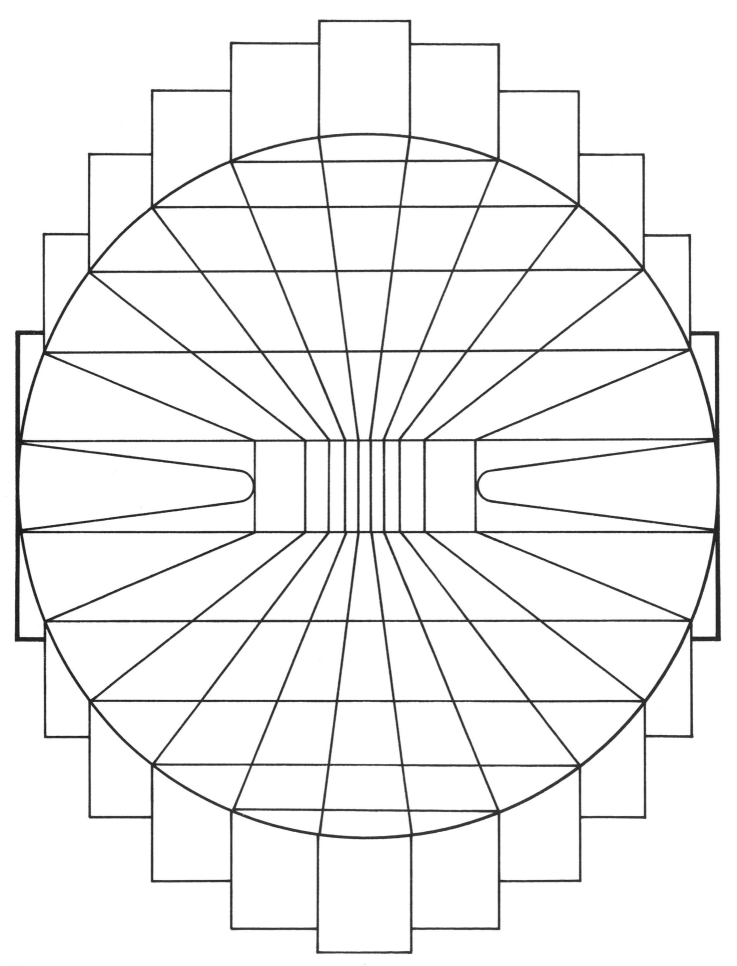

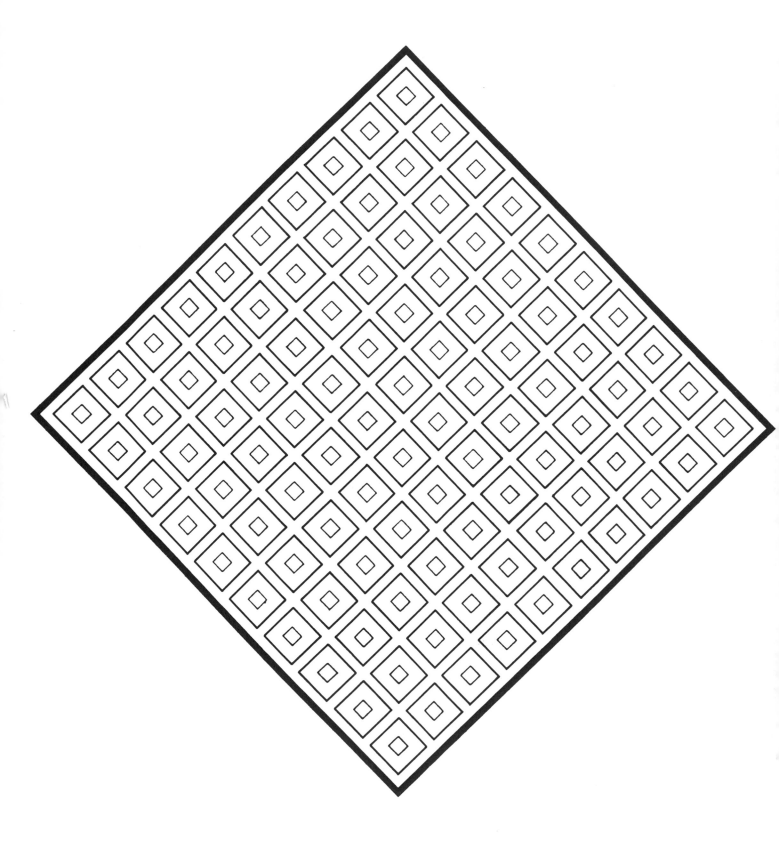

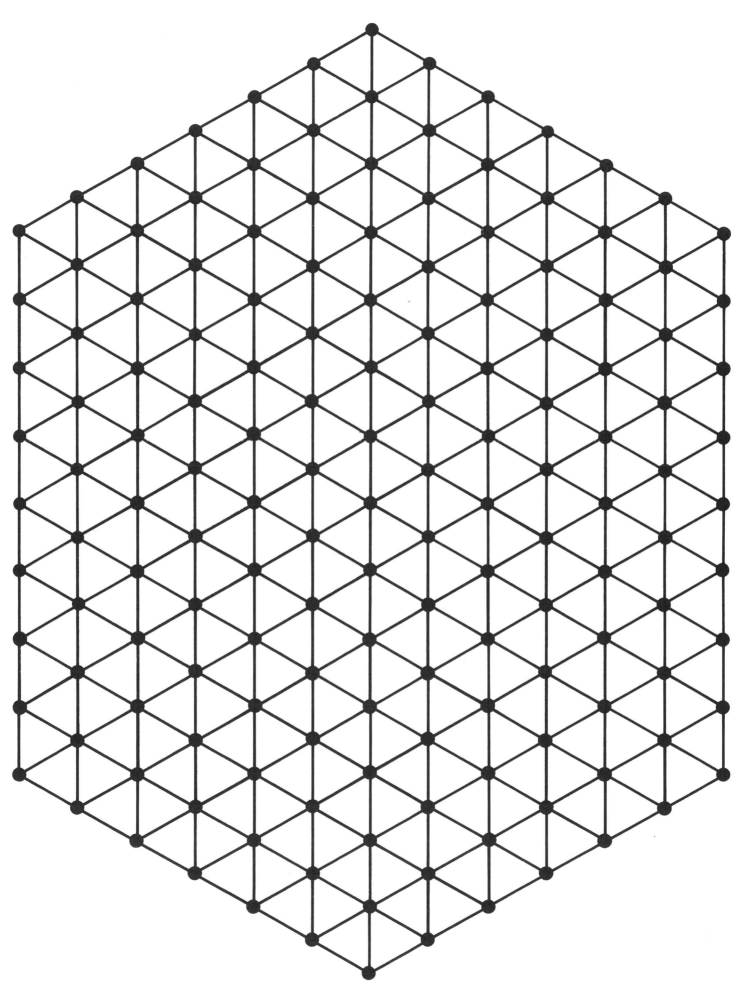

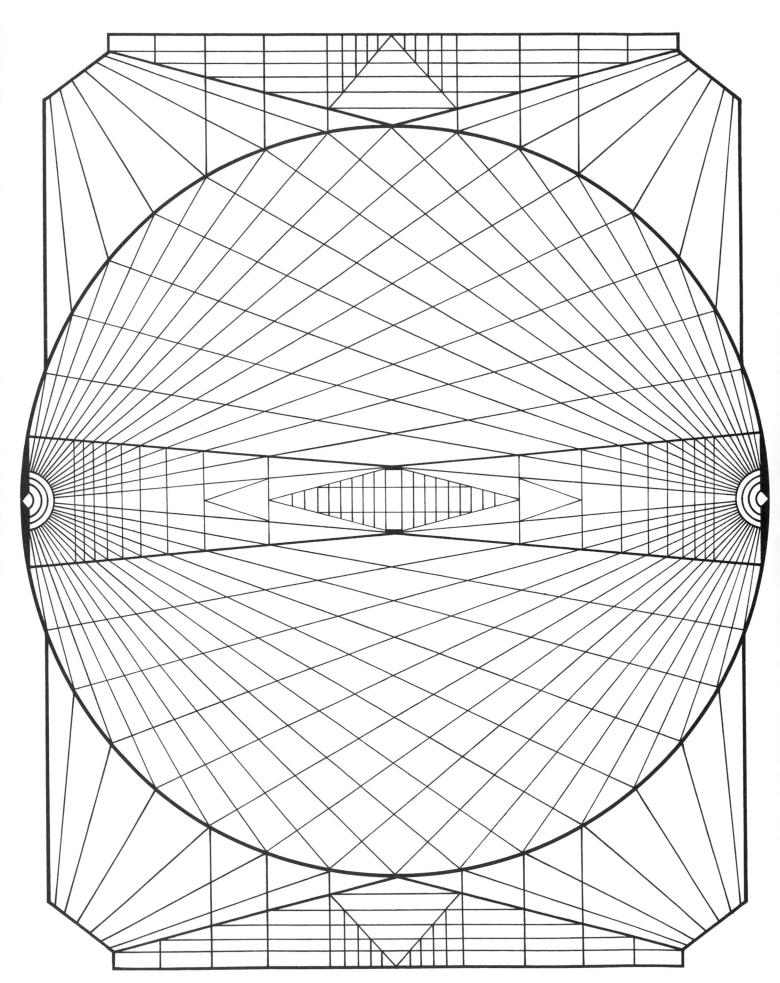

42

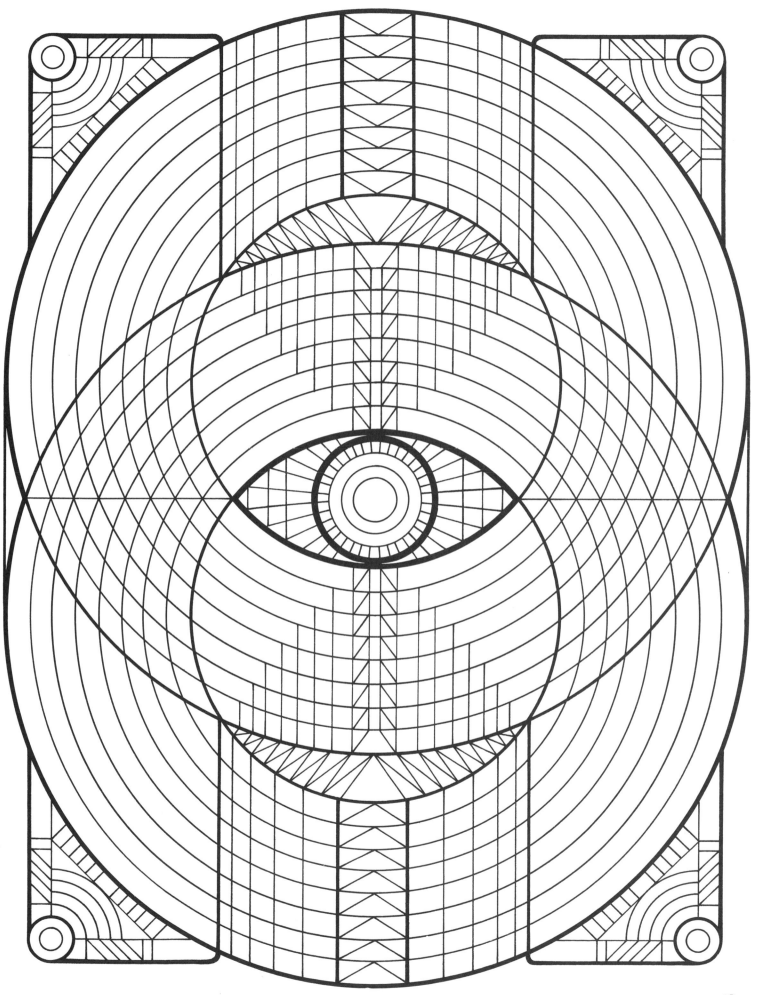

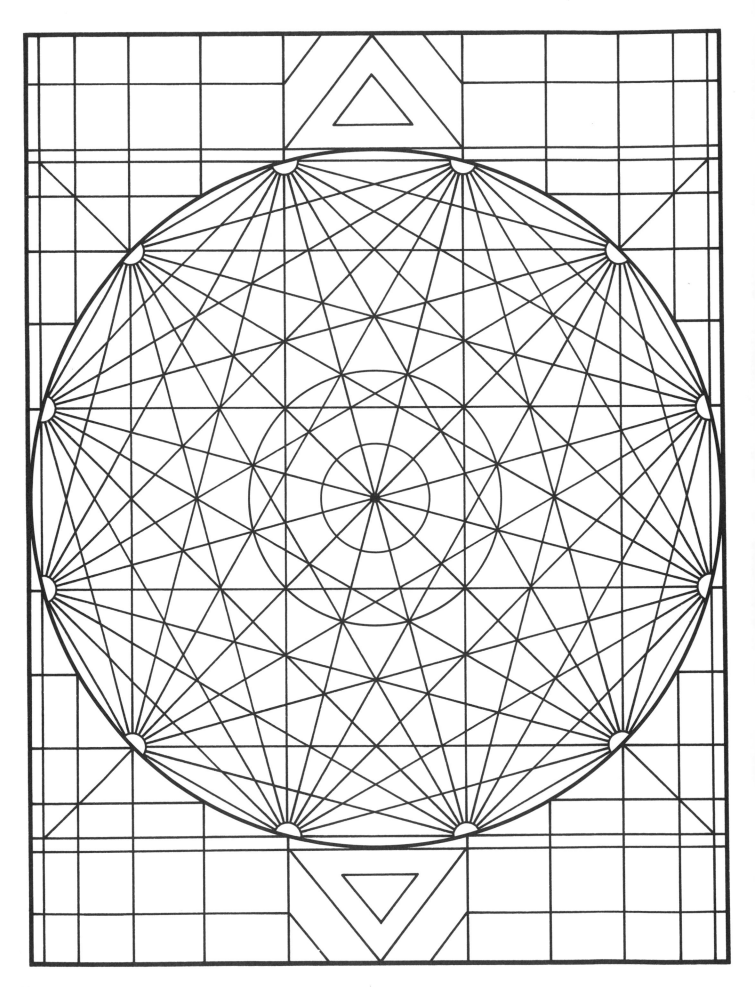

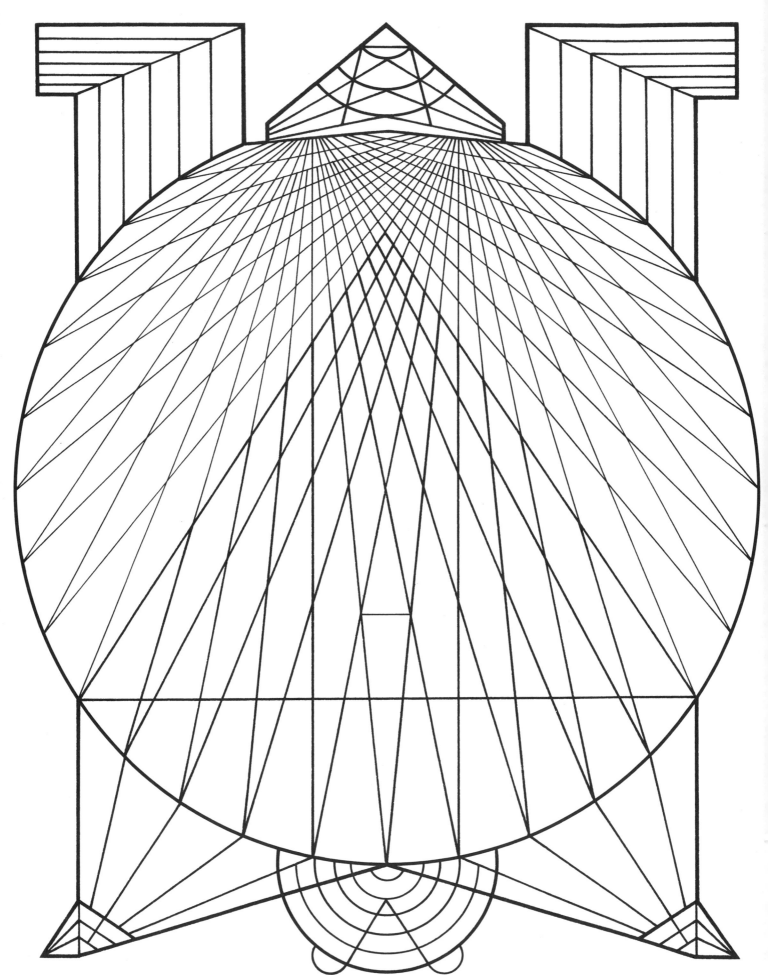